ENIGMAS *of* HISTORY

THE MYSTERIES OF EASTER ISLAND

WORLD BOOK

a Scott Fetzer company
Chicago
www.worldbook.com

World Book edition of "Enigmas de la historia" by Editorial Sol 90.

Enigmas de la historia
Los moais de la isla de Pascua

This edition licensed from Editorial Sol 90 S.L.
Copyright 2013 Editorial Sol S.L. All rights reserved.

English-language revised edition copyright 2014, 2016
World Book, Inc.
Enigmas of History
The Mysteries of Easter Island

World Book, Inc.
180 North LaSalle Street
Suite 900
Chicago, Illinois 60601
USA

For information about other World Book publications, visit
our website at **www.worldbook.com** or call **1-800-967-5325.**

Library of Congress Cataloging-in-Publication Data

Moais de la isla de Pascua. English.
   The mysteries of Easter Island. -- English-language revised
edition.
      pages cm. -- (Enigmas of history)
   Summary: "An exploration of the questions and mysteries
that have puzzled scholars and experts about the remote
location of Easter Island, including its culture, giant statues,
and writing. Features include a map, fact boxes, biographies
of famous experts on Easter Island, places to see and visit,
a glossary, further readings, and index"-- Provided by
publisher.
   Includes index.
   ISBN 978-0-7166-2665-7
1. Easter Island--History--Juvenile literature. 2. Easter Island-
-Antiquities--Juvenile literature. I. World Book, Inc.
   F3169.M97 2014
   996.18--dc23
                         2014007069

Set ISBN: 978-0-7166-2660-2

Printed in China by PrintWORKS Global Services
Shenzhen, Guangdong
2nd printing July 2016

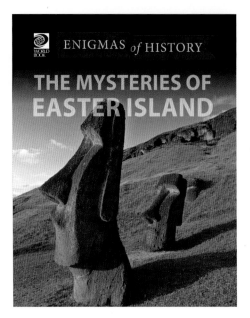

Large statues, called *moai,* were carved by the people of Easter Island between around A.D. 1200 and
1600. Such statues were carved from volcanic stone
quarried from the Rano Raraku volcano. The largest
rise as high as 40 feet (12 meters) and weigh as
much as 90 tons (82 metric tons).

© Jon Arnold Images Ltd/Alamy Images

Staff

Glossary There is a glossary of terms on page 44. Terms defined in the glossary are in boldface **(type that looks like this)** on their first appearance on any *spread* (two facing pages). Words that are difficult to say are followed by a pronunciation (pruh NUHN see AY shuhn) the first time they are mentioned.

Table of Contents

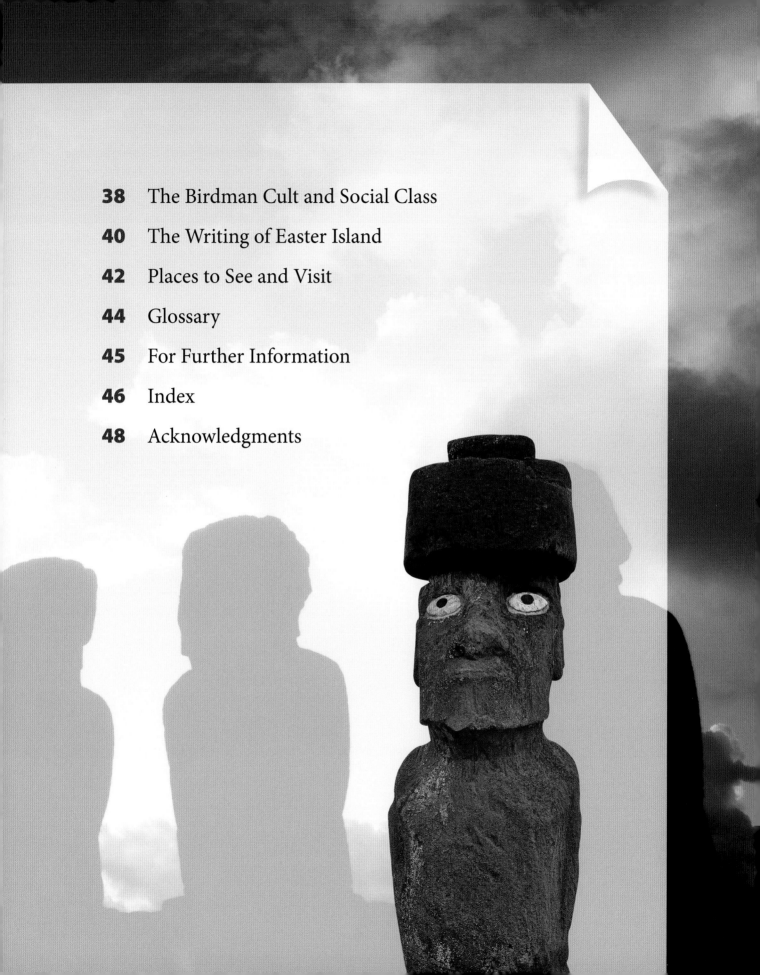

Easter Island

Easter Island is in the Pacific, some 2,300 miles (3,700 kilometers) west of South America. Since it was first encountered by explorers, this small island has dazzled the world with its natural beauty and mysterious culture. Around 900 huge stone statues dot the island and are some of the outstanding **relics** (ancient objects) of its early people.

The Navel of the World

Over time, its name has gone through many variations. The first settlers of the island called it *Te Pito O Te Henua,* which means "the navel of the world." In 1722, Dutch sailors named it Easter Island when they arrived on the island on Easter Day. The present settlers call it **Rapanui** (rah peh NOO eeh).

Location facts

Country	Chile
Capital	Hanga Roa
Population	Around 6,000 inhabitants
Density	94.9 persons per sq mi (36.6 persons per sq km)
Surface Area	63.2 sq mi (163.6 sq km)

Road
Trail or path
Urban center
Moai Zone

HANGA ROA
It is the capital and the only existing town.

SOUTH
PACIFIC OCEAN

Orongo

EASTER ISLAND

O Tu'u Hill
984 ft (300 m)

South Cape

Rano Kau
An inactive volcano is located at the island's southern end, with a lake in its crater that is 0.6 mi (0.9 km) in diameter and 919 ft (280 m) deep. The volcano is 1,063 ft (324 m) high, and its origin dates back to its eruption about 2.5 million years ago.

Statues, or Moai
The statues found farthest away from the **quarry** are usually the smallest, which suggests a relationship between a statue's size and the distance it had to be transported.

Sacred Platforms

The statues, or **moai,** on Easter Island stand on platforms called **ahu.** The ahu contain graves of the **clan** chiefs, and the statues were thought to represent the divine ancestors of the chiefs.

Maunga Terevaka

Maunga Terevaka is the largest of the island's three extinct volcanos, standing at 1,660 ft (506 m) high. It is located at the far north of the island. It has an unusual cone shape and occupies a large part of the island. Its summit is the highest point of Easter Island.

North Cape

Point San Juan

Anakena Beach

Point Rosalia

Pu'i Hill
1,049 ft (319.7 m)

SOUTH PACIFIC OCEAN

La Perouse Bay

Puakatki Volcano
1,213 ft (369.7 m)

Cape O'Higgins

Anakena Beach

In addition to its warm turquoise water and coral sand, Anakena beach is characterized by the presence of the **ceremonial** centers of Ature Huki and Nau Nau, both restored. According to Rapanui tradition, this was the place where the first king of the island, ariki (chief) Hotu Matu'a, and his people settled, arriving from a continent they called Hiva.

North

0   10,000 ft (3,048m)

Cape Cumming

Rano Raraku Volcano

This volcano, formerly known as Manunga Eo, is just 328 ft (100 m) high, and has a lake within it.

Ahu Tongariki

The largest ahu on Easter Island, with 15 statues placed on a long platform. In 1960, this ahu was destroyed by a **tsunami.** The site was later restored.

The Giant Statues of Easter Island

Easter Island is a place in the Pacific Ocean guarded by astonishing stone giants. There, one of the most isolated groups of people on Earth developed a fascinating **culture** over the centuries.

At the beginning of the 1700's, the Pacific Ocean was a stage on which human adventure played out on a grand scale. In 1722, Dutch sailor Jacob Roggeveen (1659-1729) set out on the Pacific—which was still partly uncharted—with three ships under his command. When he was nearly 2,300 miles (3,700 kilometers) from the coast of South America, Roggeveen came across a triangular island. It was Easter Sunday—April 5, 1722—when he anchored his ship in a bay on that island's north coast.

People lived on the island, but their living standard was very low. All they had to eat were chickens, mice, and the few sad vegetables that the people were able to grow. The people who lived on Easter Island could not venture out to sea to fish, because they did not have the material needed for making boats.

What most caught the sailors' attention on the island, however, were the gigantic statues, the **moai** (MOH eye), some of which were toppled over. The moai stood on large stone platforms along the island's coast. The contrast between such a poor and small population and such large statues was drastic.

Why had the statues been built? Civilizations generally make progress most quickly under favorable conditions. If they have a surplus of food, groups of humans can devote energy to tasks that are not directly aimed at survival. However, the culture of the people on this island—who called themselves the **Rapanui**—seemed to have developed under very unfavorable conditions. Either that, or the island had once been rich and later became poor. But, if that was the case, why had Easter Island become poor so suddenly?

Finally, what was the meaning of the bird **symbols** and the writing on the tablets found on the island?

LOCATION AND GEOGRAPHY

Of the names given to Easter Island in the traditional stories, the most frequently used is *Te Pito O Te Henua*, which means *the navel of the world*. The people living on the island today, however, call it

AT THE FOOT OF THE VOLCANO
At the Rano Raraku volcano, on the eastern part of Easter Island, there are dozens of large statues, both finished and unfinished. The Rapanui people got the materials they needed to make enormous statues from this volcanic crater.

Rapanui. The island's official name is Isla de Pascua, as is shown on the current maps of Chile, the country to which the island has belonged since 1888. The name is translated into other languages as "Easter Island" in English and "Île de Pâques" in French.

Easter Island, one of the most isolated lands on the planet, is located in the Pacific Ocean, about 2,300 miles (3,700 kilometers) west from the coast of Chile and 2,516 miles (4,049 kilometers) from Tahiti. Pitcairn Island, 1,400 miles (2,300 kilometers) away, is the nearest populated island, although only about 50 people live on Pitcairn. Easter Island's distance from the rest of the world adds to the mystery that surrounds it.

Easter Island has a mild, tropical rain forest climate. The island is the highest point in an undersea mountain chain that extends from east to west—the Salas and Gómez Ridge. The entire island was formed from volcanic activity. Easter Island's highest point of elevation, at Maunga Terevaka, is about 1,660 feet (506 meters) above sea level.

The island has a perimeter of 36 miles (58 kilometers) and a surface area of 63.2 square miles (163.6 square kilometers).

FIRST ENIGMAS

The Europeans who came into contact with the islanders at the beginning of the 1700's did so only for short periods of time. All who went there, however, returned knowing that they had been to an extraordinary place and seen sights that were difficult to explain. Europeans wondered how and from where the Rapanui had reached this extremely remote island. The boats and instruments for *navigating* (finding an object's position) that the Rapanui had when European explorers encountered them could never have allowed them to sail to and **colonize** Easter Island.

Another major question concerned the story behind the gigantic statues found around the island's perimeter and farther inland. Who had moved and set up these massive stones weighing several tons, and how did they do it?

Further, Europeans wondered what kind of society the Rapanui had formed that allowed them to create such gigantic monuments. And after 1722, European visitors reported that statues began to be toppled over. Why did the Rapanui begin to topple their magnificent statues?

In short, how did a small group of isolated people come to develop this great **culture** on this tiny island, and what had caused the culture's collapse?

Finally, what was the meaning of the writing found on tablets left by the culture in an earlier time?

ORIGINS OF THE PEOPLE

The location of Easter Island, halfway between South America and Polynesia, caused scientists to be uncertain about the origins of the island's people. Experts weighed evidence for both South

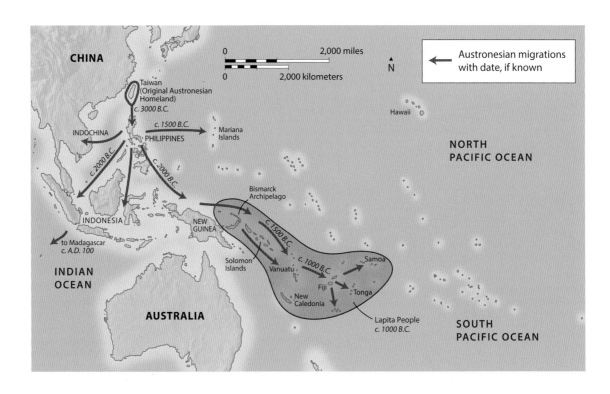

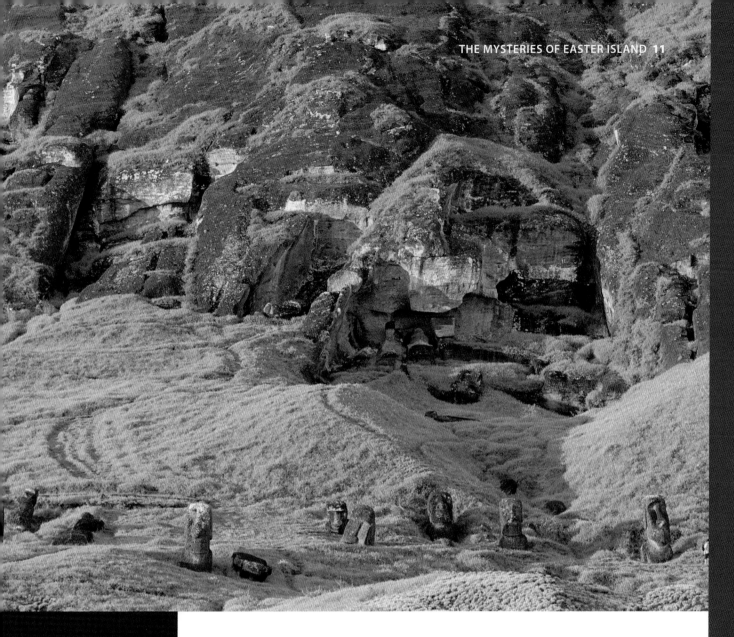

UNFINISHED
Unfinished statues sit, abandoned, on the slopes of Rano Raraku. Scientists are not certain why these statues were never finished or used.

MIGRATING TO POLYNESIA
The people who colonized Polynesia—known as **Austronesians** (AWS troh NEE zhunz)—came from Taiwan, an island off the coast of China. The Austronesians left Taiwan around 5,000 years ago.

America and Polynesia as the home from which the Rapanui traveled to reach Easter Island.

There are legends stating that the *Inca* (a South American Indian culture that founded an empire centered on Peru in the 1400's through 1532) led expeditions that could have reached some of the islands of Polynesia. However, any Indian (native American) visits to the Pacific have never been scientifically proven.

In the 1940's and 1950's, however, experts sought to prove that Easter Island had been populated by people who had traveled there from South America. A Norwegian **anthropologist,** Thor Heyerdahl, believed that the presence of such plants as the sweet potato, which originated in South America, and the similarity between some construction techniques used in certain islands of Polynesia and in Bolivia, showed that Easter Islanders came from South America.

To prove that South Americans of **pre-Colum-bian** times (prior to 1492) could have sailed the Pacific, in 1947 Heyerdahl departed from the coast of Peru on a raft of logs. The raft was as simple as any that early voyagers would have used. On this raft, *Kon-Tiki,* Heyerdahl traveled as far as the Tuamotu Islands in the South Pacific.

Scientists now know that two American crops found on Easter Island—the sweet potato and the pumpkin— were most likely brought by Polynesians from South America. This is supported by **DNA** studies done on the plants. (DNA is a thin, chainlike molecule found in every living cell on earth. Scientists can examine

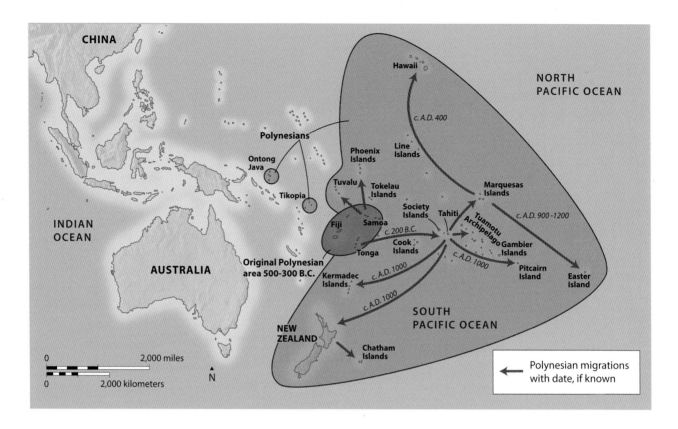

DNA to see how closely one organism is related to another.) Evidence that chickens found in South America were brought there from Polynesia supports the idea that the Polynesians brought some items back.

Heyerdahl was also convinced of the South American **colonization** of the Pacific islands because he believed that the same totora reeds that grew in South America grew in Easter Island's lagoons. Later studies of pollen—fine grains produced by male flower parts—proved that the totora reeds had come to Easter Island thousands of years before humans did, by natural means.

Scientists now believe that the travels of the Polynesians between the 900's and 1200's were part of a **migration** that had lasted for centuries. The Polynesians' double-hulled canoes with movable sails let them sail against the wind at fast speeds. Their knowledge of the sea and stars also helped them in their

navigation. It made it possible for them to colonize many Pacific islands, including Easter Island.

CULTURE—900'S TO 1600'S

Despite their isolation, the **Rapanui** experienced a **cultural** flourishing that lasted for several centuries. During this time, they had a society that was organized and **stratified.** During that time, the population grew and may have reached 10,000 inhabitants. In the early days, the **ahu** were set up: stone platforms where the celebrations of the **clans** were carried out. At first they placed small statues on the ahu, in memory of their ancestors. As the clans wanted to demonstrate their power to the other clans, they began constructing larger platforms and putting up increasingly higher and more finely developed stone statues. In ahu Tongariki there is a platform nearly 330 feet (100 meters) long where they had set up 15 statues (see pages 30-31).

MIGRATING OUT TO EASTER ISLAND

From Tahiti, Polynesians began to migrate over a large area of the Pacific. Between A.D. 900 and 1200, these peoples migrated from the Marquesas (mar KAY suhz) Islands to Easter Island.

TRADITIONAL DRESS

An Easter Islander in traditional dress.

An Easy Riddle

In hindsight, it may seem strange that anyone would think the people of Easter Island came from anywhere but Polynesia. In 1774, British navigator, explorer, and cartographer James Cook spent four days on Easter Island. To his surprise, the Tahitian member of his crew could understand the language of the Rapanui, which was similar to a dialect spoken in the Marquesas Islands. The tools used by the Rapanui—harpoons, stone hoes, tools made from basalt (a hard, dark volcanic rock), and coral files—were also similar to others used on different Polynesian islands. The fact that someone from Tahiti could understand the language of an Easter Islander should have provided a hint that the origins of the Rapanui were likely in Polynesia, and not South America.

How Did the Rapanui Reach Easter Island?

When Easter Island was first encountered by Europeans in the 1700's, major questions were raised about its people. When would they have arrived? Was there evidence of their Polynesian heritage?

Thanks to their advanced knowledge of **astronomy** and ocean currents, to the presence of certain fish and plants floating in the water, to the clouds accumulated around the mountains, and to the flight patterns of birds, Polynesians were able to explore and **colonize** many islands dispersed throughout the Pacific. Observing the sun during the day and the stars and planets during the night allowed the Polynesians to navigate their voyages. They charted a map of more than 200 stars. Another key to their success was the type of vessel they used, a double-hulled canoe—known today as a catamaran—that had great speed. The Pacific voyages of the ancestors of the Polynesian sailors began some 5,000 years ago, as people known today as **Austronesians** left the island of what is now Taiwan, off the coast of China, to migrate to new islands. In this first wave of colonization, they settled such Pacific islands as Fiji, Samoa, and Tonga. The second wave began about A.D. 400 and included present-day New Zealand, Hawaii, and the Marquesas Islands. The people who migrated to New Zealand became known as the Maoris (MOW reez).

In just a few hundred years, the Polynesians colonized several Pacific *archipelagos* (groups of islands), including a small, isolated piece of land located in the far southeast corner of the Polynesian triangle: Easter Island. Experts believe that most of the settlers on Easter Island arrived from the Marquesas and Mangareva islands. Colonizing islands on the open sea is risky and dangerous. But, the Polynesians were often forced to take that risk. Most of the islands colonized by the Polynesians are small and would soon have become much too crowded. People were forced to look for new places to live.

AUSTRALIA

What Were the Polynesian Boats Like?

According to **Rapanui** tradition, Hotu Matu'a, the first supreme chief of Rapa Nui, reached the island between the A.D. 800's and 1000's There were two voyages, one led by him and the following one by Ava Rei Pua, his sister. These voyages were most likely made on double-hulled canoes, similar to those used in the rest of Polynesia. On Easter Island there are two *petroglyphs* (carvings in rock) representing these voyages.

INFORMATION

62 ft 4 in
(19 m)

17 ft 8 in
(5.3 m)

PACIFIC OCEAN

EASTER ISLAND

The Kon-Tiki

Norwegian explorer Thor Heyerdahl became famous for the *Kon-Tiki* expedition in 1947. He crossed the Pacific Ocean on *Kon-Tiki*—a raft made of wood and other plants and natural materials from South America. The trip started in Peru and ended in the Tuamotu Islands. Heyerdahl's goal was to show how, in the past, **pre-Columbian** people of the Americas could have reached Polynesia.

Thor Heyerdahl
(1914-2002)

Heyerdahl led a six-person expedition on a journey of 4,360 miles (7,451 kilometers). In addition to rough seas encountered on the trip, the boat was frequently circled by sharks, and several of the crew were injured by moray eels.

Sergio Rapu
(1949-)

Born on Easter Island, this local **archaeologist** was the director of the island's Museo Antropológico Padre Sebastián Englert between 1975 and 1990. In 1978, Rapu made a discovery: The stone statues of Easter Island originally had inlaid **obsidian** and coral eyes, though these had disappeared over time. He made the discovery while restoring the Nau Nau **ahu** on Anakena beach.

KON-TIKI
Heyerdahl traveled from Peru to Polynesia on this raft.

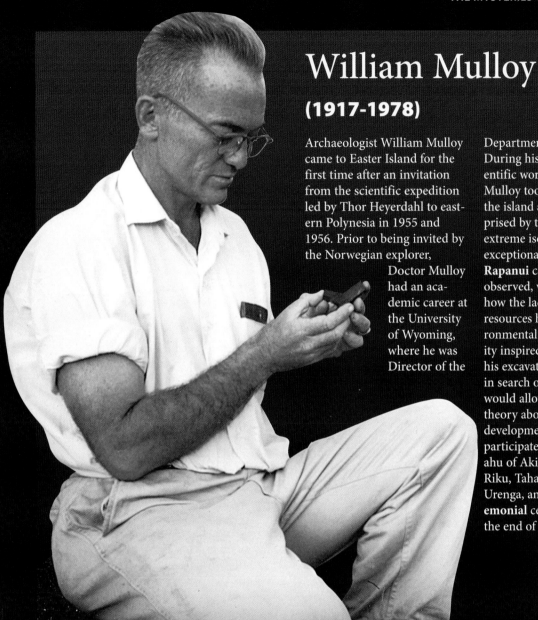

William Mulloy

(1917-1978)

Archaeologist William Mulloy came to Easter Island for the first time after an invitation from the scientific expedition led by Thor Heyerdahl to eastern Polynesia in 1955 and 1956. Prior to being invited by the Norwegian explorer, Doctor Mulloy had an academic career at the University of Wyoming, where he was Director of the Department of **Anthropology**. During his five months of scientific work on Easter Island, Mulloy took a great interest in the island and its people, surprised by the conditions of extreme isolation in which the exceptional **culture** of the **Rapanui** came about. He also observed, with keen interest, how the lack of natural resources hinted at past environmental changes. His curiosity inspired him to continue his excavations for many years in search of evidence that would allow him to form a theory about the cultural development of the island. He participated in restoring the ahu of Akivi, Vai Teka, Ko Te Riku, Tahai, Vai Uri, Huri A Urenga, and the ahu of the **ceremonial** center of Orongo at the end of the 1970's.

Jacob Roggeveen

(1659-1729)

A Dutch sailor who, on April 5, 1722, discovered Easter Island during an exploration trip intended to research Pacific islands. Roggeveen's purpose was to find Davis' Land—a land that was thought to exist only because a British pirate had described it as being across from the coast of Chile—and later to reach the also assumed South Land (Terra Australis, or Zuidland) following the instructions of Willem Schouten, a sailor who had thought that it was found near the Tuamotu Islands. Roggeveen left Holland in 1721 with three boats and a crew of 270 men.

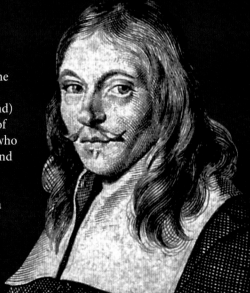

How Were the Statues Made and Transported?

No one knows for certain what system was used by the natives of Easter Island for putting up and moving their mysterious statues. But, experts believe the Easter Islanders could have used wooden sleds and strong ropes.

One of the mysteries related to the stone statues, the one that has led to the most debate among specialists is how the statues were moved, or transported. There are several different theories on the matter.

Easter Island contains around 900 giant moais. Only 288 of them were connected with some type of **ahu,** the **ceremonial** platforms of the distinct **clans,** which were generally located along the coast. More than 400 statues did not make it out of the place where they were being carved, the **quarry** of Rano Raraku volcano (see pages 8-9). The rest were found scattered over the island. Some figures stand at the sites where they were placed, and others were abandoned for various reasons during transport. Those that remained in the quarry are the greatest source of information on reconstructing the sequence of their creation, given that many were left unfinished during different stages of production. Some stone statues were abandoned shortly after the sculptors began, while others were finished and ready to be transported to their intended site.

THE WORK PROCESS

The work began with carving out a block of **tuff** (rock made out of volcanic ash and other volcanic fragments) the size of the planned statue. Tuff was used because it was soft and easy to carve.

The statues were carved lying face up. The carving process began with the area around the sides of the rock selected to be carved. There was a 2-foot (0.6-meter) channel around the rock where the sculptors stood to work. This allowed several quarry workers to carve the head—in which the ears and nose were emphasized— arms, hands, and the rest of the body at the same time.

The tools used by the **artisans** (skilled workers) for sculpting were principally **adzes** made of **basalt,** a volcanic rock much harder than the tuff being carved. Remnants of many of these tools were found at Rano Raraku.

Once the statue was finished, it was cut from the mountain by removing the remaining stone piece that had kept it connected it to the rock. Then there was the work of transporting it. In many cases, these heavy rock statues were moved long distances.

POSSIBLE TRANSPORT TECHNIQUES

Over the course of time, the **Rapanui** probably developed different techniques for transporting the statues,

Rano Raraku **Quarry**

There are a total of 397 unfinished statues in the crater and surrounding slopes of the Rano Raraku volcano. These include "The Giant," a statue 68 feet 11 inches (21 meters) tall and not yet detached from its rock base. Why did the Rapanui carve the statues inside the crater, and not on the slopes, when it is evident that it was much more difficult to remove the sculptures from the crater? Were the statues not intended to be moved from there? The only thing that is certain is that most of those lying inside the crater are smaller and less decorated than those on the slopes.

BURIED
Over time, earth has covered the statues that were left unfinished in Rano Raraku.

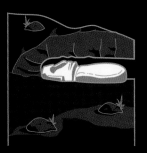

The Process

Entire mountains were removed to create the giant statues of Easter Island. The volcanic rock was cut with **basalt** tools, and the statues were shaped while still in the **quarry**. Regarding the transportation, there are several theories: one maintains that the statues were moved face down, using a wooden sled; and another proposes that they were placed upright and moved using ropes and **levers**.

1 CHISELING THE STATUES
The statues were carved face up in the volcanic rock. A statue's back was not carved.

2 TRANSPORT
The statue was loosened from the surrounding rock and dragged with ropes down the slope to the foot of the volcano.

3 DIGGING THE PIT
It was dragged to a pit formed for setting the statue upright, and placed with the help of plant-fiber ropes and wooden levers.

THEORY A: FACE-DOWN TRANSPORT

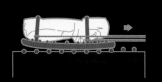
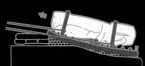

THEORY B: UPRIGHT TRANSPORT

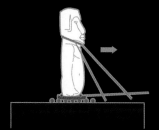

6a TRANSPORT
The statue was transported face down, on a wooden sled which was pulled over wooden logs.

7a PLACEMENT
Upon its arrival at the ahu, rocks were placed below the statue to raise it to the level of the pedestal.

8a LIFTING
With the help of levers, more rocks were placed under the statue to form a mound, enabling it to be raised up.

6b TRANSPORT
A wooden sled was placed under the base of the statue, and it was balanced with ropes while moved.

depending on their size, weight, and the resources available. Beyond what old **Rapanui** legends describe—that the **ariki** (chiefs) transported statues with the strength of *mana* (a supernatural power or influence that flowed through objects)—according to the research the statues may have been carried either upright or face down (with plants protecting them) on wooden planks used like a sled. The sled was pulled by ropes. It slid over wooden poles placed under the sled to reduce friction.

The **archaeologist** Sergio Rapu maintains, however, that statues were moved upright, or in a vertical

position, following the tradition that the statues "walked," while other researchers believe that this may have depended on the size of the statue. The Rapanui must have used levers and plant-fiber ropes throughout the process, especially when lifting the figure up to the platform. After the statue was in place, **artisans** placed coral eyes in the sculpture. The engraved decorations on the back were also carved after the figure was placed on the **ahu.** There are many indicators that the *pukao* (top piece) was also added at the end, while the statue was atop the ahu. Pukao cylinders, carved from the Puna Pau **quarry,** measure

between 3 to 7 feet (0.9 to 2.1 meters) high and 7 to 10 feet (2.1 to 3 meters) in diameter.

To test theories regarding the transportation of the Easter Island statues, scientists have tried to move statues under similar conditions. One experiment consisted of placing a statue in a vertical position on a wooden sled, which was then dragged over rails with lubricated supports or over fixed crossbeams with little friction. Another alternative placed the statue face down on a sled with the base toward the front, dragging it over parallel poles. With the help of ropes and levers, 50 or 60 people could have

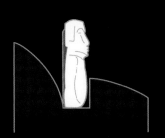

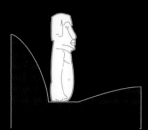

4 POLISHING THE BACK
Since only the front and sides had been cut, the neck and back had to be filed down, which reduced its weight.

5 OPENING THE PIT
The statue was freed from the hole to continue the move, flattening the ground in front.

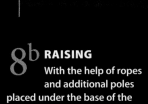

7b PLACEMENT
Once the statue was successfully brought to the ahu, they prepared to raise it to the platform.

8b RAISING
With the help of ropes and additional poles placed under the base of the statue, it was raised up onto the ahu.

9 THE CROWNING
Once the statue was set upright on top of the ahu, the mound of rock was removed and they began the "dedication" of the statue. The last details were carved in the back and face, coral was set in the eyes, and the statue was crowned with a pukao (a hat or headdress made of red stone).

moved one multi-ton statue. Czech engineer Pavel Pavel and American archaeologist Charles Love successfully tested these two alternatives in the 1980's.

In 2011, archaeologists Terry Hunt and Carl Lipo moved a statue in an upright position, rocking it from side to side to shift it forward. In this experiment, 18 people were required to shift a 10-ton (0.9-metric-ton) replica of a statue.

LAKE
Located inside the Rano Raraku crater, totora reeds grow along the banks of this freshwater lake.

Raising the Statues

Provided the statues were not moved in an upright, walking fashion, they would have needed to be lifted from a horizontal to vertical position. These images show one theory as to how that might have been accomplished.

THE LEVERS

One or several levers were slid in between the ramp and the statues on each side. Using these levers, the statues would lean closer and closer toward the platform.

STONE RAMPS

Once the statue was transported to the **ahu,** the **Rapanui** may have gradually lifted it by piling up stones below the structure, which would have formed an increasingly high ramp. The operation would have been completed with wooden **levers,** the other key element in the lifting process. Building the ramps meant a lot of extra work for the Rapanui, both during the lifting phase and once the statue was in place and the ramp had to be removed.

Coronation of the Statues

Most researchers believe that the pukao—carved from the Puna Pau crater (photo at left)—were put in place once the statues were already on the ahu. However, Mulloy and others propose that they would have raised the statue with it already attached.

CONTROL
Specialized **artisans** who were among the noble class managed the work progress.

Anatomy of the Statues

The statues of Easter Island share many characteristics, but no two are exactly the same. All of them are carved out of volcanic rock (around 800 are made of **tuff**), they are usually crowned with a headdress (pukao) made of red scoria (a porous volcanic rock), and they sometimes have eyes made of coral and **obsidian** (a natural glass formed from lava flows that cooled quickly).

Distribution

Of the nearly 900 statues on Easter Island, 397 are found in the Rano Raraku **quarry,** 288 are associated with the **ahu,** and the rest are spread throughout the island. The majority of the ahu are on the coast, but there around 20 in the interior of the island.

Orientation
The ahu are placed so that their statues have their back to the sea and they are facing the village of their descendants—since it is thought that they are statues of dead leaders.

Coral and Obsidian Eyes
All of the statues with obsidian and coral eyes—or, in some cases, painted eyes—have been restored. Before 1978, when **archaeologist** Sergio Rapu and associate Sonia Haoa found the fragments of an original eye, it was not known that the sculptures had inlaid eyes.

Tahai Ceremonial Center

Tahai, the most important **ceremonial** center of Easter Island, was restored between 1969 and 1970 by William Mulloy. The site is made up of 3 ahu beside the sea: ahu Vai Uri includes the first group of statues, beside which a canoe ramp paved with stones reaches the sea; ahu Tahai, to its right, has a solitary statue without a pukao; and nearby is ahu Ko Te Riku, also with only one statue, this one with a pukao.

Statue of the ahu Vai Uri

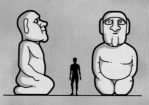

Statue of the ahu Tahai

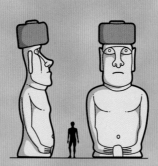

Statue of the Ko Te Riku

Paro, the tallest statue on an ahu
The Paro statue is the tallest that was ever erected on the island. It toppled over and now lies in three parts. A moai on the ahu Hanga Tetenga is a little taller, but it is known that it fell during the erecting process because the eye sockets are not open.

Information on Paro Statue

MATERIAL	WEIGHT	HEIGHT
Volcanic tuff from Rano Raraku	91.5 tons (83 metric tons)	32 ft 2 in (9.8 m) (not including pukao)

Why was the statue known as "The Giant" left unfinished?

The Giant, the largest statue on the island (70 feet [21.3 meters] tall and 270 tons [245 metric tons]), is twice as tall as the Paro, but it was never finished or erected. It lies within the Rano Raraku crater.

Ahu Ko Te Riku

Ko Te Riku was restored and is the only one standing on this ahu. Its eyes were added using material not original to the statue during restoration. It measures 17 ft (5.1 m) high. It is estimated that it was carved in the 800's A.D.

Pukao

59 **Moai** with pukao have been counted on **Rapanui.** The average weight of this headdress, which some experts say represents a hairstyle (a bun), and others a hat, is 10 tons (9 metric tons). The absence of the pukao on many Moai suggests that the feature was added later.

Eyes

The gaze **symbolized** the protection granted by the Moai. After a conflict between tribes, the Moai of the conquered tribes were knocked down and the eyes removed, to take their power from them.

Ears

In general, they are very elongated, representing those of the native people. The Moai of the earliest period had shorter and wider ears.

The Pukao Quarry

The headdresses were carved in a quarry of red scoria named Puna Pau. Some 31 pukao have been counted, spread throughout the island.

Unique Statues

Some of the 900-plus statues found on Easter Island stand out from the rest. They are distinguished by the material they are made of, their position, their features, their decoration, or their particular meaning.

Ava Rei Pua

This is one of a few statues (at right) made of **basalt;** there are only 10 on the entire island. Its torso was recovered at Anakena during the expedition of Thor Heyerdahl in 1956, while the unusually elongated head was found during the *Kon-Tiki* Museum expedition in 1987. When both parts were put together, the islanders christened the figure Ava Rei Pua, the name of the sister of Hotu Matu'a, the first king of the island, according to **Rapanui** mythology. Today, it is housed in the P. Sebastian Englert **Anthropological** Museum on Easter Island.

TUKUTURI
This statue (above) lies on the slope of Rano Raraku and is the only kneeling statue on Easter Island.

MOAI KO TE RIKU
Located in the Tahai area, birthplace of king Nga'ara, this statue (at left) has eyes of coral and red slag, which were replaced some years ago when it was restored.

TITAHANGA O TE HENUA
This statue (above) on Moto Nui, made from volcanic rock, marked the line of the territorial divisions of the **clans.**

DECORATED BACK

The back of this statue, carved with figures related to the bird-man cult, makes it a unique and very valuable piece. It dates to A.D. 1000, although it is believed that the designs were added later. It was painted red and white, but the pigment has been lost.

MASCULINE AO (CEREMONIAL OAR)

RAA (RAYS OF THE SUN)

FEMININE AO (CEREMONIAL OAR)

POKI-MANU (BIRD-CHILD)

VIE-MANU (BIRD-WOMAN)

TANGATA-MANU (BIRDMAN)

OMOTOHI (FULL MOON)

UA (RAIN)

HA-NUA-NUA-MEA (RAINBOW)

MATA-MATA-IKA (HAIL)

Hoa Hakananai'a

Although it is believed that it was originally outdoors, this statue (above) was found in a house in the **ceremonial** center of Orongo in 1868, by the crew of the British ship H.M.S. *Topaz*. The statue was transferred to London, with the help of the islanders, and today is part of the collection in the British Museum. It weighs 4 tons (3.6 metric tons) and measures about 8 feet (2.5 meters) tall. Its name means "the stolen friend" in the Rapanui language. Chile has demanded its return several times.

What Was the Significance of the Statues?

According to the most widely accepted theory among experts, the statues represented ancestors and acted as a **symbol** of the power of the law that brought unity to the **clan.**

The extraordinary features of the stone statues were not limited to their size. It is also necessary to understand the important role they filled in the society of Easter Island. Its people gave them special value as a *symbol*—something that stands for or represents something else, especially an idea, quality, or condition. It appears that statues were put up in honor of a notable historical figure or figure from **Rapanui myths** and represented the spirit of an ancestor who, in this manner, was present among the people to guide them.

The statues gained their significance when they were placed on an **ahu,** the **ceremonial** platform built by the **clan,** facing the houses of the community, making its members feel protected. Their gaze projected the mana, that is, the spirit of the ancestor from which the clan believed that power and intelligence flowed. These statues were constructed in the period known as Ahu Moai (A.D. 1000-1500), the era when a religion-based political system dominated Easter Island society, based on the cult of ancestor worship common throughout Polynesia.

The social structure created on Easter Island was a positive system there. The **ariki** (king or high chief of Easter Island), supported by the upper class of priests and high-born families, settled issues involving the interests of the various clans.

CHANGE OF VALUES

With no internal conflicts and with social **stratification** (a society with higher and lower classes), the Rapanui society developed more advanced agriculture and architecture. The accumulation of a food surplus allowed many to devote themselves to sculpting and transporting statues. As time passed, the association with ancestors declined in importance, and so instead the statues that represented them became mainly a symbol of the strength and power of the clans. Clans became the focus of the population's social structure.

This process of change in the symbolic value given to the statues developed along with other changes in Rapanui society. As resources for survival became more scarce, and clans no longer felt protected by the aristocracy, the clans began to compete among themselves for survival.

The construction of large statues reached its peak at the end of the 1600's, then declined, and in the end about 600 statues were abandoned in the Rano Raraku quarry. These statues have proved useful in helping to unlock at least some of the mystery of the statues and Rapanui culture.

Social Order

The leader of each clan was the ariki, the chief of the tribe who represented the family of the most revered ancestors. Next were the priests (ivi atua), the warriors (matato'a), the expert **artisans** (maori), the family patriarchs (tangata honui), the common people (hurumanu) and the servants and slaves (kio). Rapanui society was organized under a unique form of religious monarchy. The family of the ariki were also the source of knowledge and mastered **Rongorongo** script, a system of engraving using **obsidian** spikes or shark's teeth on wooden tablets.

PUKAO

The most popular theory is that the pukao represented a hair treatment practiced on Easter Island that included smearing the hair with red volcanic rock. It could also depict some type of ceremonial hat.

THE CLANS

The highest level of social organization achieved by Rapanui society was that of the clans, or mata. It is estimated that there were up to 12 clans divided into two groups. The limited amount of soil suitable for growing crops caused serious conflicts over control of these lands.

CONFEDERATIONS AND CLANS

■ Mata Tu'u Aro

■ Mata Tu'u Hotu Iti

Were "Long Ears" of Incan Origin?

According to explorer Thor Heyerdahl, the long ears of some Rapanui showed that the first migratory wave to arrive on Easter Island was from the **Inca** Empire, given that the Quechuas—Indians of the dominant group of the Inca empire—had this characteristic. However, Heyerdahl's theory now has less weight. A new theory states that the elongation of the ears was a sign of prestige on Easter Island. To achieve this, heavy discs were inserted into the earlobes, stretching them with their weight.

The Tongariki Ahu

Although its statues were toppled—some during the civil wars that took place on Easter Island from the 1500's onward, and some in 1960 by a **tsunami** (a series of powerful ocean waves produced by an earthquake)—this **ahu** was reconstructed by specialists from the University of Chile in the 1990's. Today it can be seen in its full splendor.

Back Against the Sea

The Tongariki ahu is located in Hanga Nui, on the northeast coast of Easter Island. Its central platform measures 315 feet (96 meters), and the entire ahu measures 490 feet (149 meters). When they were originally made, all of the statues probably had a pukao, but only one was replaced in the restoration.

COLOSSAL SIZE Near the Rano Raraku volcano, the Tongariki ahu is the largest stone monument in all of Polynesia.

Why Were the Statues Destroyed?

Toward the end of the 1600's, different **clans** within Easter Island society had disputes over such natural resources as farmable land and wood, which were becoming scarce. Many of the stone statues, **symbols** of the society, were destroyed when society became less stable.

The construction of statues ordered by the different clans of **Rapanui** society created a race to see who could build the largest sculptures. This was the state of the culture in the late 1500's, when the deterioration of the island's land began to make it more difficult to grow enough food for the people. With boats, the Easter Islanders might have been able to move to another island. However, as there were now few trees on the island, the Rapanui no longer had enough wood to make the large rafts needed to leave the island. Rivalry between the clans became worse.

THE MONARCHY'S END

The power of the religious monarchy, with its priestly class, was replaced by an upper class military, the *matato'a* (warriors). A legend still repeated today illustrates the source of the conflict. It describes this crisis as the explosion of the vengeance of a powerful woman who was extremely angry because she did not receive her share of a large lobster.

The struggle for survival increased violent behavior. In order to avoid violence, the weakest members of the clans took refuge in underground caves. The outbreak of tension not only devastated the rival clans, but also their symbols, the stone statues.

The destruction of the statues began around 1680 and continued through the early 1800's.

The destruction of the statues was not always caused by conflict. Once the meaning of the stone statues was lost from the culture, the clans themselves, urged on by other needs, used the ahu platforms for other purposes, such as graves, and destroyed the statues connected to them. When the first Europeans arrived in 1722, some of the statues had already fallen. At that time, more than a century had passed since the Rapanui stopped carving the statues.

How Many Inhabitants Lived on the Island?

The first estimate was made by missionaries who arrived on the island in 1864. They calculated that there were some 2,000 inhabitants. In 1877, there were only 110. It is said that the population at one time reached 15,000, a figure that dropped drastically after the internal conflicts. Diseases brought to the island by Westerners also took a toll on the size of the population.

Environmental Archaeology

The analysis of **fossilized** particles of **pollen** found on Easter Island was key to discovering the existence of completely different plants from those that are currently found on the island.

Reconstructing the Environment

Palynology (the study of fossilized particles of pollen) allows the reconstruction of the *flora* (plant life) of a specific place in the past. Thus, scientists can get information about the climate, the soil, and even the lives of the people who lived in a place, because plants make up part of the food people eat. This is possible because the exterior shell of pollen is very hard and can survive for tens of thousands of years. In the case of Easter Island, the pollen analyses conducted by John Flenley and Sarah King showed that the island once had a thick subtropical forest. The most abundant species would have been the Easter Island Palm—now **extinct**—a tree with tall trunks topped by fan-like leaves. Easter Island also had such trees as the toi, toromiro, and hauhau, in addition to ferns and other shrubs.

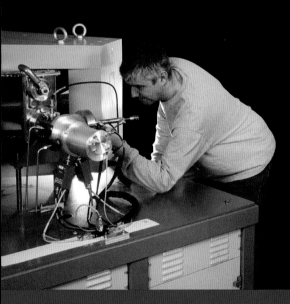

^{14}C

CARBON 14
The age of each layer of sediment which has pollen grains is found using **radiocarbon dating** (a process used to determine the age of an ancient object by measuring its radiocarbon content).

THE LOST FOREST
Researchers John Flenley and Sarah King extracted a *sediment column* (a column of the matter that had settled in the water) from Rano Kau lake. The pollen grains in the column revealed the existence of a palm forest. The researchers learned from the sediment layers that the palms disappeared about a thousand years ago.

Flora Evolution

Over the last 38,000 years, there have been great variations in the plant life on Easter Island. In prehistoric times, there were extensive forest zones, particularly in areas around the main volcanoes of the island. During the last 1,000 years, the Polynesians, and later the Europeans, introduced new species, which make up the plant life found on the island today.

800's TO 1000's
With the arrival of humans to the island, such species as the taro, sweet potato, sugar cane, and pumpkin were introduced.

1000's TO 1500's
Different theories arise to explain the extinction of the native palm tree. Some scientists believe slash-and-burn farming, and others believe the introduction of rats to be the cause.

Pollen Samples

The Rano Kau volcano, currently inactive, is located at the extreme southeast end of Easter Island and reaches an altitude of 1,063 feet (324 meters). Its crater measures almost a mile in diameter, and within it is a lake some 820 feet (250 meters) deep. The fossilized pollen samples that revealed the existence of plants no longer found on Easter Island were taken from the bottom of the lake.

POLLEN GRAIN
Enlarging a microscopic grain allows scientists to identify its species.

1700's

Little ground cover remains on Easter Island. The forests that survived to this time are basically toromiro (illustration), mako'i , and hauhau, the species that may have been used to make the ropes to transport the statues.

1800's - PRESENT

European plant species are introduced, and livestock farming begins, which speeds the disappearance of native plants. Today Easter Island has such foreign species as eucalyptus, melia, and toroko, which were introduced in recent years. The mauku piro is also spreading.

Later History of Easter Island

Beginning in the 1600's, the **Rapanui** had to cope with many difficult changes. Western explorers came to the island, eventually causing the population of the small island to be victimized by ranch owners and Western diseases. Harm done to the environment of Easter Island was equally serious.

1680'S THROUGH 1700'S

In the later phase of Easter Island's history, beginning in the 1600's, construction of the statues stopped, and those that had been set up began to be knocked down. The **ahu** that had been used to hold statues were modified and covered by collective graves, known as *avanga.* That solution was adopted out of necessity when Easter Islanders could no longer continue burning corpses because firewood had become so scarce. Overpopulation used up the resources of the island, and an unstoppable chain of events followed. The destruction of trees and other plants made it even harder to grow food crops because the volcanic land, deprived of its plant cover, no longer held water. Production from orchards and fields fell considerably.

The struggle for food triggered violent clashes between the 12 **clans** of Easter Island, who allied with one of two major groups. Their structure became more and more military. They not only crushed their adversaries, but also demolished the **symbols** that represented them: their **moai.** The women, children, and the physically weak sought refuge in caves. There was a great environmental crisis, despite the effort they had put into maintaining the productivity of the soil, using technological advances that demanded even greater efforts than constructing and transporting statues.

The greatest impact was seen in the loss of trees, which made it so that ahu, statues, and canoes could no longer be built. The Rapanui adapted to the new conditions, both economically and in their changed ideas.

1800'S THROUGH MODERN TIMES

In 1862, an international company, The Society of the Seven Friends, composed of Chilean and Peruvian industrialists, recruited the Rapanui to work on various ranches in Peru. Of the 2,000 Rapanui who left the island around that time, only 15 survivors returned. Many of them contracted smallpox, tuberculosis, and other diseases that transformed into epidemics and brought the islanders close to **extinction.** In 1877, there were only 110 inhabitants remaining on the island. The territory became part of Chile in 1888, and the Rapanui population only regrouped and revived as a **culture**—a culture focused on tourism—toward the middle of the 1900's.

In 1966, during the presidency of Eduardo Frei Montalva (1911-1982), what is known as the Easter Island Law was issued, which recognizes the residents of the island as Chilean citizens and establishes rights and responsibilities for them. At that time, a government was set up, as well as various public services from the Chilean State. The law also openly acknowledges the complexity of the administration of the territory of Easter Island. Some reasons include the island's exceptional **archaeological** wealth; its geographic isolation; the level of civil involvement desired by the native Rapanui; and the loss of a great number of Easter Island's inhabitants during the 1800's, when they were taken to perform manual labor in Peru. Rapanui professor Alfonso Rapu (1942-   )—the older brother of Sergio Rapu (see page 16)—exercised a key leadership role in the movement that led to the law.

Probably the most remarkable change was the process of integration into the modern world that began at that time. Currently, the Rapanui admit to having given up self rule, but they also maintain that they have not given up ownership of their land. The descendants of the Rapanui consider themselves Chileans, but also the true owners of the land of their ancestors. As they see it, the land is essentially a resource belonging to the extended family group, not subject to individual ownership.

TOPPLED STATUES
Researchers maintain that many of the statues were knocked down by the islanders themselves in the period after construction was halted in the second half of the 1600's.

The Birdman Cult and Social Class

The changed **Rapanui** society of the 1700's called for a new system of **symbols.** What developed was a set of festive **ceremonies** and competitions that determined on an annual basis who retained power.

In the basalt rocks of Orongo, a village located on the edge of the Rano Kau crater, there are representations of the birdman (Tangata Manu): 110 illustrations in all. But, what does this character signify? Why does it appear?

Experts believe Rapanui society was damaged and shocked when the warriors took power. The increase in **obsidian** weapons dating to this period is likely evidence of a more violent time.

Worship of ancestors was left behind and a new social order began. As farmland became poorer and poorer, the Rapanui had to enclose spaces with rocks, creating stone-walled gardens that held in humidity and protected crops from the wind. In addition to these technical means of improvement, they turned to magic to help the harvest, to aid poultry fertility, and to ensure good fishing.

THE RITUAL IN ORONGO

During this period that began at the end of the 1600's—a time known as Huri **Moai** (the toppling of the statues)—political power was no longer inherited. It was earned through a ceremony that took place at Orongo. The ceremony, organized in spring, celebrated fertility and selected the birdman, the person who would become the absolute authority on the island for the following year. The selection was made through competitions. The winner of the competitions trial automatically became the chief and holder of the mana, which granted knowledge and power. As a symbol of the birdman's new status, the winner shaved his head and painted it white and red. He would have spent six months preparing himself to perform his duties. If he was a member of the **clans** from the northeast, he would spend that time in Anakena; if he was from the clans of the southeast, he went to Rano Raraku.

The last known birdman was called Rukunga, and he lived during the second half of the 1800's.

The Ceremonial Village

The new order of the Huri Moai period needed unified power based on strength, not on the moral prestige of the chiefs and its priestly class. Thus, the ceremonies were held in a central location, the village of Orongo, located on the narrowest edge of the Rano Kau crater. Its houses, facing the sea, were made of basalt tiles.

HOMES
The floor was shaped like a rectangle with rounded corners. The walls were with made from thick, double tile filled with soil and rocks.

PETROGLYPHS
Petroglyphs (paintings and engravings in stone) show Orongo's importance in island life. They include images of the birdman, birds, and fish.

What Was the Significance of the Orongo Ceremony?

We do not know exactly when the birdman ceremony began, its link with the creator god Make-Make is unclear, and there is not much certainty regarding exactly what it meant to the winning or losing clans. The ceremony was a competition in which the participants had to descend a cliff in Orongo, swim the channel that separated the islet of Motu Nui from Easter Island, and bring back an egg of the sacred manutara bird, a species of tern. This ceremony was held in early spring. The winning clan held political and religious power on the island for one year.

The Writing of Easter Island

The Mysterious **Rongorongo**

Known by the name **Rongorongo,** the **hieroglyphs** (writing in which picture **symbols** represent ideas and sounds) found on Easter Island have been the object of many hours of research. Today, however, their meaning and origin are still unknown. According to local legends, the king Hoto Matu'a brought 67 tablets in Rongorongo to the island and was able to read and write the characters on them. However, the first Europeans to land on Easter Island—a fleet from Holland in 1722—did not note any evidence of these carvings. Neither did the Spanish in 1770 or British naval captain James Cook (1728-1779) in 1774. A French missionary, Eugène Eyraud (1820-1868), was the first to refer to Rongorongo in writing in 1864, explaining that in Rapanui houses there were tablets or sticks with several kinds of hieroglyphic symbols. The 25 known tablets written in Rongorongo contain 14,000 different glyphs. Swiss language expert Alfred Métraux (1902-1963) and German expert Thomas Barthel (1923-1997) reached the conclusion that there are around 120 basic elements that, combined, can form between 1,500 and 2,000 compound symbols.

MEANING

The French missionary Eugène Eyraud pointed out that, according to the native people, the tablets contained religious songs and prayers.

The Materials: Wood, Stone, and Bones

The choice of materials used for engraving the **symbols** in Rongorongo was linked to the material resources available to the Rapanui on Easter Island. The majority of these **hieroglyphic** symbols are carved on makai and toromiro wood, and they are found to a lesser extent on rocks, fish bones of considerable size, or the bones of marine mammals—all durable materials. When wood started to become scarce, in the late period of the history of the Rapanui, the settlers of Easter Island retrieved floating pieces of driftwood to continue the tradition of writing.

TABLETS
Twenty-five wooden tablets, engraved on both sides with chips of obsidian (a natural glass formed from lava flows that cooled quickly), bird bones, or shark teeth, were found on Easter Island.

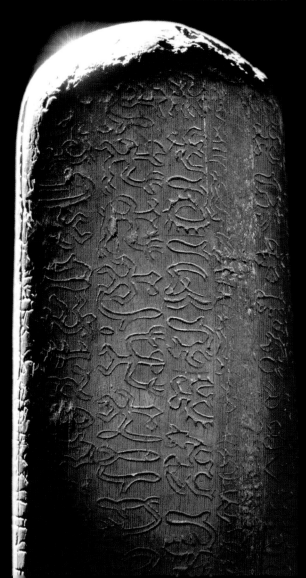

So Few Examples

One reason scholars may continue to have a difficult time deciphering Rongorongo is the lack of examples of the hieroglyphs. There are only about two dozen objects with the script of Easter Island on them. In 1868, the Roman Catholic Bishop of Tahiti, Bishop Jaussen (1815-1891), received a gift from the recently converted people of Easter Island—a piece of rope made of hair entwined around a tablet covered in Rongorongo writing. Jaussen asked the priest on Easter Island to send him any other examples he found. The priest found three more tablets to send to his bishop. A lay brother on Easter Island earlier in the 1800's had reported seeing thousands of examples of the writing. Where did they all go? Since the 1800's, about 18 more tablets have been found. None of them are on Easter Island today. They are scattered in museums around the world.

Places to See and Visit

OTHER PLACES OF INTEREST

MUSEO ANTHROPOLOGICA PADRE SEBASTIAN ENGLERT

EASTER ISLAND, CHILE

The museum collects, preserves, and researches the **archaeological** heritage of Easter Island and its people. Related to this mission, it houses a specialized archaeological and bibliographical collection and promotes understanding of the **Rapanui** culture. It is 20 minutes by foot from the center of Hanga Roa (it is recommended to walk along the coast, through the commercial center of Tahai). There are guided excursions of the island that include the museum, which can be seen in one hour.

RAPA NUI NATIONAL PARK

EASTER ISLAND, CHILE

Because of its volcanic origin, Easter Island has unique flora that includes 34 plant species, and animals including the notable Manutara, or spectacled and sooty tern, and diverse fish species. This national park has great archaeological value because of the abundance of pictographs, petroglyphs, **moai,** and **ahu.**

Hanga Roa

THE CAPITAL

Hanga Roa is the only city on Easter Island. It has a port, and it is where practically all of the administrative and leisure activities on Rapanui are concentrated. Its residents represent nearly 85 percent of the island's population. As the island is small, the places of interest are very close to the capital.

ON THE OUTSKIRTS

Very close to Hanga Roa, barely a mile away, is the ceremonial center of Tahai. The complex allows you to see three ahu (ceremonial platforms) in a single visit: the ahu Vai Uri, the ahu Ko Te Riku, and the ahu Tahai. Building the three platforms themselves, not including the statues they sustained, required more than 2,000 tons (1,813 metric tons) of stone and soil.

Orongo

Orongo is the most significant **ceremonial** center on Easter Island and is found barely 3.7 miles (6 kilometers) from the city of Hanga Roa. Various **ceremonies** related to the birdman cult, central to the culture of Easter Island, were practiced in this village, which was built very close to a cliff. Some ancient houses, whose interior walls bear painted symbols, are preserved in Orongo. There are also numerous outdoor petroglyphs.

BRITISH MUSEUM

LONDON, UNITED KINGDOM

This prestigious museum holds the famous statue Hoa Hakananai'a, one of the few existing tattooed statues. The statue is notable because of the quality of the carving of the basalt and because it combines traits of the two phases of Rapanui prehistory: the classic style on its front, and the many **symbols** of the new order carved on its back.

NATIONAL MUSEUM OF NATURAL HISTORY, SMITHSONIAN INSTITUTION

WASHINGTON, D.C.

A stone figure taken from Easter Island in 1886 remains in the Smithsonian.

Glossary

Adze — Axelike tools.

Ahu — Platforms on Easter Island, on which, at one time, moai were erected.

Anthropologist — Scientist who studies humans and human cultures.

Archaeologist — One who scientifically studies the people, customs, and life of ancient times.

Ariki — Chiefs on Easter Island.

Artisan — A skilled worker.

Astronomy — The study of the universe and the objects in it, such as stars and planets.

Austronesia — The islands of the south and mid-Pacific, such as Indonesia, Malaysia, and the Philippines.

Basalt — A hard, dark volcanic rock.

Ceremony — A special form or set of acts to be done on such occasions as weddings, funerals, or holidays.

Clan — A group of people who are related through a common ancestor.

Colonize — To leave one's country and settle in another land.

Culture — A way of life for humans. Every human society has a culture, which includes a society's arts, beliefs, customs, institutions, inventions, language, technology, and values.

Extinct — when every member of a *species* (kind) of living thing has died.

Flora — Plant life of an area.

Fossilized — Hardened remains or traces of an animal or plant of a former age.

Hieroglyph — A form of writing in which picture symbols represent ideas and sounds.

Lever — A rod or bar that rests and turns on a support called a fulcrum. A force of effort is applied at one end of the rod to lift a load placed at the other end.

Migration — Moving from one place to another.

Moai — Giant stone statues carved and placed by the Rapanui people of Easter Island.

Myth — A legend or story, usually one that attempts to account for something in nature. Most myths express a religious belief of a people and are of unknown origin.

Obsidian — A natural glass formed from lava flows that cooled quickly.

Pre-Columbian — Of or belonging to the period before the arrival of Columbus in the Western Hemisphere (1492).

Quarry — A place where stone is dug, cut, or blasted out for use in building.

Radiocarbon dating — A process used to determine the age of an ancient object by measuring its radiocarbon content. The radiocarbon, or carbon 14, in the tissues of a living organism decays extremely slowly, but it is continuously renewed as long as the organism lives. After the organism dies, it no longer takes in air or food, and so it no longer absorbs radiocarbon. The radiocarbon already in the tissues continues to decrease at a constant rate. This steady decay at a known rate—a half-life of approximately 5,730 years—enables scientists to determine an object's age.

Rapanui — The people who developed the culture of Easter Island; also, that culture's word for Easter Island.

Relic — Ancient object.

Rongorongo — Hieroglyphics of the Rapanui people.

Slash-and-burn farming — A practice used by some farmers wherein an area is cleared by cutting down trees and vegetation and burning them. The ashes help fertilize the soil.

Stratified — A culture divided into different classes of people, for example, stone carvers, farmers, and chiefs.

Symbol — Something that stands for or represents something else, especially an idea, quality, or condition.

Tsunami — A series of powerful ocean waves produced by an earthquake, landslide, or volcanic eruption.

Tuff — Rock made out of volcanic ash and other volcanic fragments.

For Further Information

Books

Arnold, Caroline. *Easter Island: Giant Stone Statues Tell of a Rich and Tragic Past*. Clarion Books: New York, 2004. Print.

Barron, T. A., and William Low. *The Day the Stones Walked: A Tale of Easter Island*. New York: Philomel, 2007. Print.

Capek, Michael. *Easter Island: Unearthing Ancient Worlds*. Minneapolis: Twenty-First Century, 2009. Print.

Reis, Ronald A. *Easter Island*. New York: Chelsea House, 2011. Print.

Riggs, Kate. *Easter Island*. Mankato, MN: Creative Education, 2009. Print.

Websites

"Beneath Easter Island." *National Geographic Channel*. NGC Europe Limited, 2013. Web. 07 Feb. 2014.

Dangerfield, Whitney. "The Mystery of Easter Island." *Smithsonian.com*. Smithsonian, 1 Apr. 2007. Web. 07 Feb. 2014.

"Easter Island." *History.com*. A&E Television Networks, 2014. Web. 05 Feb. 2014.

"Hoa Hakananai'a." *The British Museum*. Trustees of the British Museum, n.d. Web. 07 Feb. 2014.

"World History: Easter Island Statue." *BBC*. BBC, 2014. Web. 07 Feb. 2014.

Index

Acknowledgments

Pictures:

© AGE Fotostock

© Nicolás Aguayo (www.aguayo.cl)

© Alamy Images

AP Photo

© The Trustees of the British Museum

© Stéphane Compoint

© Corbis Images

© Getty Images

© Brigid Mulloy Collection

© Museo Antropológico P. Sebastián Englert, Isla de Pascua

© Nederland Scheepvaartmuseum Amsterdam

© Pitt Rivers Museum – University of Oxford

© Photo Sebra Film, Sweden

© Sergio M. Rapu

© Scala Archive

© Science Photo Library

© Thinkstock